To order additional copies of this book, contact:
Xlibris Corporation
1-888-795-4274
www.Xlibris.com
Orders@Xlibris.com

For My Daughter Bethany

Starters / Light lunches

Apple soup	15
Crab and salmon lasagne with avocado	8
Deep fried Brie with blueberries	9
Garlic prawns, goats cheese and apple with a lemon dressing	10
Pears in Parma ham with a honey and balsamic reduction	11
Port and Stilton with mulled wine	13
Quail breast in quail broth	14
Rabbit pâté	16
Scallops in honey and ginger	12
Seafood medley	19
Smoked pheasant, ginger 'air' and sweet potato	18
Tea ham	17

Fish

BBQ monk fish, Jerusalem artichokes, baby spinach and sautéed potatoes	27
Buttered cod, chicory and broccoli puree	26
Cider battered haddock, 'tartared' peas and chips	21
Crispy Calamari with lime dipping sauce and hot and sour dipping sauce	25
Gurnard, pickled beetroot and cannelloni	24
Mackerel, bruschetta, asparagus and apple with fennel sauce	22
Octopus and stuffed squid open pie	29
Paella	23
Roast brill, fried mushrooms, new potatoes and a spicy BBQ sauce	30
Sea bass in a herb crust, lemon rice, honey and mustard broccoli and spinach	28
Trout in a pepper, melon and coconut sauce with samphire and fondant potatoes	31

Meat

Beef burger, cheddar and balsamic chutney, oven chips	36
Ham, chicken, mushroom and banana pizza with a barbecue base	32
Lasagne	34
Peppered steak, green beans and sweet potato	35
Pork loin fillet with apple, butternut squash and broccoli	33
Rack of lamb, plum sauce, mash potato and garlic carrots and baby sweet corn	38
Roulade of pork, orange sauce and sweet potato	37

Chicken

Caramelised duck, roasted dumplings, carrots and green leaf puree	40
Chicken dhansak with fragrant rice	45
Chicken Kiev, sweet corn and muffin potatoes	46
Chicken, spring onion and pak choi kebab with satay sauce	39
Deep fried chicken strips with a lemon sauce and sweet and sour sauce	43
Lime chicken, coconut rice and papaya salsa	42
Roast Chicken, gingered leek, red cabbage and parsnips	44

Desserts

Amarasu	48
Flambé banana with brandy caramel	47
Ginger and mint cheese cake	50
Hazelnut and honey parfait, rose jellies and vanilla caramels	55
Mango and toffee meringues	54
Peach and chocolate mousse in chocolate cups	51
Strawberry and vanilla cheese cake	53
White chocolate parcels with berries, thyme and mint	52

Dave Rook - Something Special

A huge thank you to Chris, Mal, mum and Linda (second mum) for proof reading and for taking responsibility for all the errors in this book (joke)! Thank you to Pete for spending so much time on the photo's and to everyone who helped and tasted the recipes in this book but especially my wife Susan for proof reading the book, tasting the dishes and most importantly for putting up with me! She has suggested that I dedicate this book to our daughter Bethany; I dare not argue! Bethany, this book is for you.

I hope you enjoy this book but please see it as an expression of thoughts and ideas I have had. I want you to change the recipes in this book to suit your own tastes and to share your new ideas with others. All of the recipes, measurements, sizes and quantities are to be seen as a suggestion on how to cook the meal, not as an exact step by step guide.

I would also like to point out that I have not gone (as so many other chefs have) for authenticity with these dishes. For example, the pizza in this book is not what one may consider to be 'traditional'. The traditional pizza has influenced the dish and although most of the pizza's I've had from restaurants or takeaways are soggy and greasy, they're not without their good points. The same applies for Indian and Chinese dishes; I have allowed the UK versions to influence me greatly because I believe this is our culture and reflective of the period in which we live.

www.daverook.com

Starters / Light lunches

Crab and salmon lasagne with avocado

Deep fried Brie with blueberries

Garlic prawns, goats cheese and apple with a lemon dressing

Pears in Parma ham with a honey and balsamic reduction

Scallops in honey and ginger

Port and Stilton with mulled wine

Quail breast in quail broth

Apple soup

Rabbit pâté

Tea ham

Smoked pheasant, ginger 'air' and sweet potato

Seafood medley

Crab and salmon lasagne with avocado (4 people)

You will need:

200g dressed crab, 200g smoked salmon slices, ½ avocado (flesh only, skin and stone removed), 2tsp crème fraiche, 2g chopped chives plus extra for decorating, 1 small finely chopped shallot, ¼ very finely chopped mild green chilli (deseeded) and 1tbs olive oil.

In a saucepan, gently cook on medium low heat 1tbs olive oil and 1 finely chopped shallot for about 5 minutes then add ½ avocado flesh and ¼ finely chopped mild green chilli. Cook for a further 5 minutes.

Add 2 tsp crème fraiche with a few good twists of black pepper and cook for another 5 minutes. Using a potato masher, mash until fairly smooth (but not pureed). Add 2g chopped chives and mix.

To serve, make the tower by building it like a lasagne; With the aid of a chef ring (optional), start off with a thin layer of salmon, then put on top 1 ½ tsp crab meat. Repeat until you've used 4 slices of Salmon and 3 tsp of crab meat (I used one layer of salmon, crab, salmon, crab, salmon, crab, salmon).

Add 1 ½ tsp avocado mix on top.

Garnish with a small strip of chive.

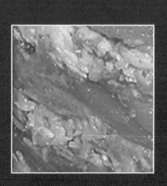

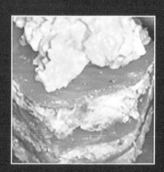

Deep fried Brie with blueberries (2 people)

You will need:

2 x 100g pieces of Brie, 100g blueberries, ½ tbs caster sugar, 1 beaten egg, 4tbs type OO flour, 3 slices of white bread blended into bread crumbs, a small handful of crushed walnuts.

Add 3 slices of white bread into a blender and blend until it becomes bread crumbs. Add a small handful of crushed walnuts and set aside on a plate.

In a saucepan, cook the 100g blueberries on low-medium heat with a splash of water and ½ tbs caster sugar until it becomes jam like (do not let it boil).

First roll the 2 x 100g Brie in a total of 4tbs type OO flour, then roll in 1 beaten egg and then in the bread crumbs. Put into fridge to rest for at least 30 minutes.

Cook the Brie in a deep fat fryer for about 2 - 3 minutes at 180°C.

Serve with 1 - 2tbs of blueberry sauce.

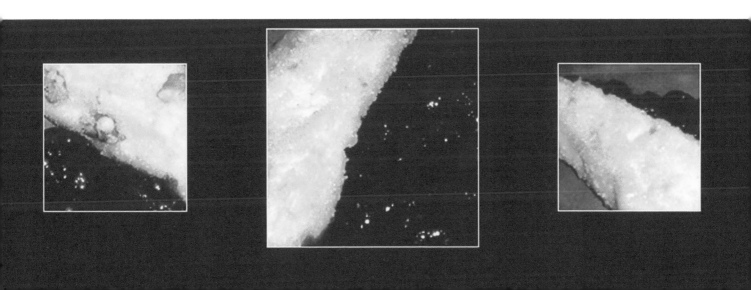

Garlic prawns, goats cheese and apple with a lemon dressing (4 people)

You will need:

3 finely chopped garlic cloves, ½ tsp cornflour, half finely chopped and deseeded mild green chilli, 1tsp honey, 30ml olive oil, 6 tiger prawns, 1 lemon, 10ml white wine vinegar, 1tsp caster sugar, 2 basil leaves, 100g goats cheese, 1 green apple, a handful of pea tops

Prepare in advance:

De-shell 6 tiger prawns (leaving the tail) and remove the vein along the back. Wash the prawns thoroughly.

Make a corn starch paste by mixing ½ tsp cornflour and 1tbs water.

Core the apple, then cut ½ of the apple into 16 pieces.

To make the lemon dressing, add the juice of 1 lemon into a pan and bring to a simmer, then turn off the heat and add 20ml olive oil, 10ml white wine vinegar, 1tsp caster sugar and 2 very finely chopped basil leaves.

In a frying pan, add 10ml olive oil and when hot, add 3 finely chopped garlic cloves and half a finely chopped and deseeded mild green chilli. After 20 seconds, add the prawns. Turn when the underside is pink. After 30 seconds, add the cornstarch paste and 1tsp honey. 30 seconds later, turn off the heat. Mix round and try to coat all the prawns evenly.

To serve, scatter a few pea tops around the plate, place 4 thin slices of apple in the middle, a few pieces of the goats cheese and place the garlic prawns on top. Drizzle 2 – 3 tsp of lemon sauce around the pea tops.

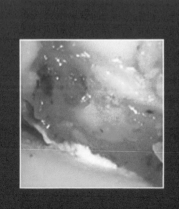

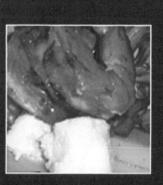

Pears in Parma ham with a honey vinaigrette (4 people)

You will need:

2 cored and halved pears, 1 ½ tbs balsamic vinegar, 1tbs set honey, 3tbs extra virgin olive oil, 4 roughly chopped sage leaves, 12 sheets of Parma ham, pepper, a few lettuce leaves.

Set the oven to 160°C.

Core 2 pears and halve each. Lay down 2 sheets of Parma ham and place a pear half in the middle. Add a few chopped sage leaves and a twist of black pepper. Bring the sides of the Parma ham in and then lie the third sheet of ham over the top and wrap round.

Cook for 12 – 15 minutes.

In a saucepan, add 1tbs set honey and 3tbs extra virgin olive oil. Bring to a medium heat and stir until the honey has been absorbed. Add 1½ tbs balsamic vinegar and turn heat to low.

Drizzle a generous amount of the vinaigrette across the plate, put a lettuce leaf in the corner and the pear in the middle so a corner is on the leaf.

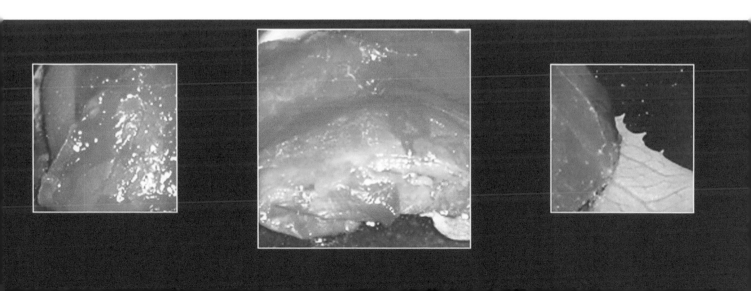

Scallops with ginger and honey (2 people)

You will need:

6 washed scallops, 7g sliced root ginger, a little ginger powder, a little paprika, a little ground cinnamon, pepper, 5tbs honey, 2tsp olive oil, 1 slice of white bread.

Prepare in advance:

Wash the 6 scallops and marinade in 7g sliced ginger and 5tbs honey for 1 hour.

Toast 1 slice of white bread until lightly golden.

Add 2tsp olive oil to a frying pan and when the oil just begins to smoke, add the 6 scallops (with as little marinade as possible), cook for approximately 1 ½ minute, then turn over and cook for another 1 minute and add the remainder of the marinade to the frying pan.

To serve: whilst the scallops are cooking, cut the toast into slices and place on a plate. Sprinkle a light amount of pepper, paprika, ginger powder and ground cinnamon around the toast and plate. Remove scallops place onto the toast and then pour the ginger and honey mix over the top.

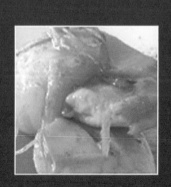

Port and Stilton and Mulled wine (4 people)

You will need:

8 crackers, 1 red onion, 20g butter, 150ml port, a small wedge of good quality Stilton, 100ml orange juice, 100ml cranberry juice, 100ml full bodied red wine, 5 cloves, 1" cinnamon stick, ½ nutmeg, 1 star anise, 2tbs caster sugar

Prepare in advance:

In a large jug, add 100ml orange juice, 100ml cranberry juice, 100ml full bodied red wine, 5 cloves, 1" cinnamon stick, ½ nutmeg and 1 star anise. Leave for 24 hours, remove the cinnamon stick and then leave for another 24 hours.

Add mulled wine to a saucepan and bring to the boil then add 1-2tbs caster sugar (to taste) and allow to simmer for 15 minutes.

Whilst the wine is simmering, slice 1 red onion into thin rings and sweat with 20g butter in a low-medium heat pan for about 10 – 15 minutes. Then turn the heat up to full, keep stirring, and when the pan is hot add 150ml port.

Keep the heat on high and cook until all the port has thickened and been absorbed by the onion (3 - 5 minutes). Transfer the red onion to a plate.

Spoon 1tsp of the onion onto a cracker with a large dice sized cube of Stilton cheese and put into the oven at 180°C until the cheese has just melted

Serve with the warm mulled wine in shot glasses

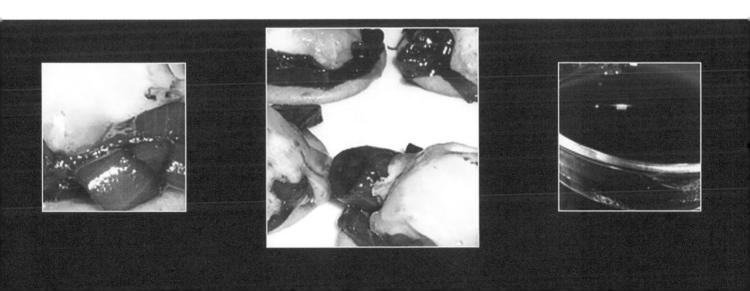

Quail breast in quail broth (2 people)

You will need:

2 quails, 230g celery, 150g carrot, 30g bunashimeji mushrooms, 3g thyme leaves, 2 bay leaves, ½ nutmeg, 1tbs olive oil, ½ white onion, 25g butter

Prepare in advance:

Remove breasts from both quails and season breasts with a tiny amount of salt and pepper.

In a large saucepan, add 200g roughly chopped celery, 100g roughly chopped carrot, 2 bay leaves, ½ nutmeg, ½ white onion and 1tbs olive oil and sweat for 5 minutes (with lid on) on medium heat. Add the breast-less quails and brown for 5 minutes. Add 900ml of water and cook with lid off on a gentle boil for about 45 minutes.

After 45 minutes drain and reserve the liquid (discard everything else). Return to a medium heat and whilst the liquid is simmering gently add a few twists of black pepper, 30g diced celery, 50g diced carrot and cook for 15 minutes. Add 3g thyme leaves, 30g bunashimeji mushrooms and cook for a further 10 minutes.

During the last 10 minutes, get a frying pan hot and add the 4 quail breasts with 25g butter. Cook for about 5 minutes each side or until your liking.

If being served as a starter, place the breasts on the plate and drizzle the broth around the side. If as a light lunch, add mash potato.

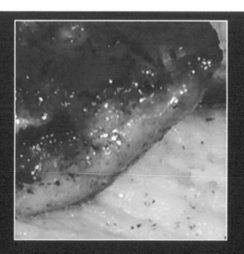
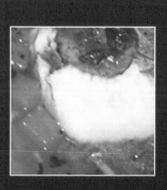

Apple soup (4 people)

You will need:

4 cored and peeled apples, 2 chopped carrots, 2 chopped leeks, 1 chopped potato, 1 chopped tomato, 1 chopped sweet potato, 3 whole garlic cloves, 2 chopped celery sticks, 1 sprig of rosemary, 1tbs honey, 1tsp finely ground black pepper, 6 cloves, a few fresh chopped sage leaves, ½ nutmeg, 2tbs olive oil.

Prepare in advance:

Make a vegetable stock by browning 2 chopped carrots, 2 chopped leeks, 1 chopped potato, 1 chopped tomato, 1 chopped sweet potato, 3 whole garlic cloves, 2 chopped celery sticks and 1 sprig of rosemary, 2tbs olive oil in a saucepan (there is no need to peel the vegetables). After 10 minutes, add 1 litre of water. Boil until halved, then remove vegetables but squeeze all liquid out. Strain again.

Add 6 cloves and ½ nutmeg into an infuser and add to the stock.

Add 4 cored, peeled and chopped apples with 1tsp finely ground black pepper and 1tbs honey to the stock.

Allow all to simmer for about 30 minutes.

Remove the infuser and puree until smooth. Add the infuser and continue for another 15 minutes. Then, puree again.

Add a few fresh chopped sage leaves and serve hot, with fresh bread.

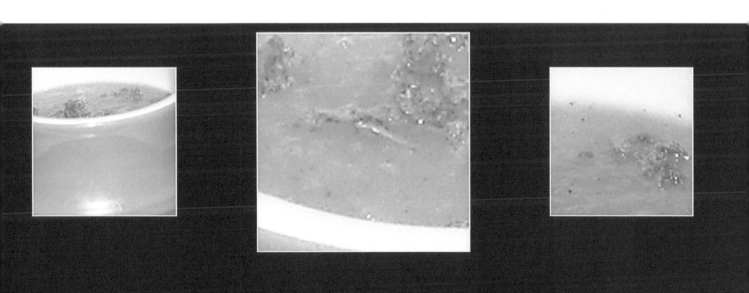

Rabbit pâté

You will need:

250g rabbit meat, 100g chicken liver, 200g mince pork, 4g fresh rosemary leaves, 2 garlic cloves, 1 shallot, 80g chestnut mushrooms, 1 egg, 75ml dry apple juice, 1tbs double cream, lots of bacon (I used about 14 rashers of smoked bacon) , 20g strasberries and a few extra for decoration (these are a cross between strawberries and raspberries - you can use raspberries instead), ½ tsp salt

In a food processor, slowly blend 250g rabbit meat, 100g chicken liver, 200g mince pork and 4g rosemary leaves until well combined and no large lumps of meat remain. Reserve.

Blend 2 garlic cloves, 1 shallot, 80g mushroom, 20g strasberries, 1 egg and ½ tsp salt in a food processor. Add this to the meat and add 75ml dry apple juice and 1tbs double cream. Mix well!

Line the inside of an oven proof dish (similar size to a small bread tin) with bacon and then spoon in the pate. To decorate, put a few more strasberries and a sprig of fresh rosemary on top. Put a lid on top and cook in oven at 180°C for 1 ½ hours. Allow to cool and it's ready to eat!

To serve we found it went best with chive infused ciabatta toast.

Tea Ham

You will need:

        1kg gammon (shoulder), 10 cloves, 10 black peppercorns, 10 tea bags, 2tbs caster sugar, 1tbs honey

Add to a large pan of cold water 10 cloves, 10 black peppercorns, 10 tea bags, 2tbs caster sugar, 1tbs honey and then bring to the boil; as the water boils the tea bags will create a scum so as soon as it starts to boil remove the pan from heat. Allow the water to boil for 1 minute then remove and discard the tea bags as well as any froth or scum that has appeared.

Add 1kg gammon ham and simmer for 1 and half hours.

Drain and allow to cool then serve with a crisp green salad.

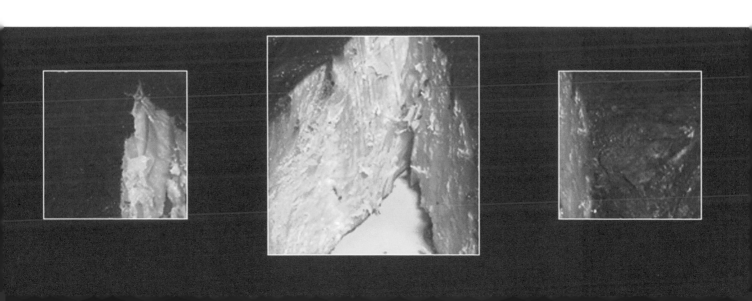

Smoked pheasant, ginger 'air' and sweet potato (4 people)

You will need:

20g chopped ginger, ½ tsp lecite, 1 sweet potato, ½ tbs truffle oil, 1 level tsp honey, 2 pheasant breasts, 1tbs olive oil, a handful of pea tops, 1 finely chopped shallot, a stove top smoker.

Add 18g chopped ginger to 250ml water and bring to boil for 10 minutes, or until reduced by half. Blend until smooth. Add ½ tsp lecite to the liquid and whisk to form a froth. This is the 'air'. When whisking, you may need to tilt the bowl and keep spooning off (and reserving) the 'air' as it appears. You only need a total of 2 - 3tbs of 'air'.

In a frying pan, gently cook 1 finely chopped shallot and 2g chopped ginger until soft. Reserve.

Wash and peel the sweet potato and slice 16 x 2mm discs. Reserve discs for later. Chop the remainder of the sweet potato and boil for 30 minutes. Drain, add ½ tbs truffle oil, 1 level tsp honey and the ginger and shallot mixture. Blend to make a smooth sauce.

Slice 2 pheasant breasts into thin strips and sauté in 1tbs olive oil for 3 - 5 minutes over a medium-high heat. Then transfer to a smoker and smoke with hickory wood chips for 10 minutes to finish off the cooking.

Add the sweet potato discs to the frying pan and sauté in the pheasant juice for 5 -7 minutes or until crispy

To serve: I spoon the ginger 'air' around the side of the plate, added a small handful of pea tops to the middle, place the sweet potato discs around and then place half a pheasant breast in the middle on top of the pea tops. I spoon a thin layer of the sauce on top of the pheasant.

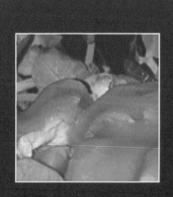
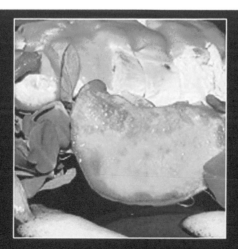

Seafood medley Starter / light lunch (2 people)

You will need:

1 lemon grass stick, 2 king scallops, 2 baby squids sliced into 3 rings, 4 peeled and cleaned prawns (keep the shells), 90ml double cream, 2tsp Worcestershire sauce, 5g fresh chopped tarragon, 1 very finely chopped shallot, 10g butter, 1tbs extra virgin olive oil.

Prepare in advance:

To make the kebabs slice one lemon grass in half lengthways, then skewer (in order): squid, scallop, prawn, squid, scallop, prawn, squid. Repeate for the second kebab. Leave in fridge for 20 minutes before cooking.

In a saucepan, add the prawn shells and heads with 50ml water and cook the prawns until liquid has reduced by half. Discard the prawns and sieve the prawn liquid. Add to the prawn liquid 10g butter and 1 very finely chopped shallot cook in a saucepan until the onion is soft. Reduce heat to lowest and add the 90ml double cream, 2tsp Worcestershire sauce and 5g chopped tarragon.

Take the shellfish off the lemon grass stick. Get a frying pan fairly hot with 1tbs extra virgin olive oil and add the scallops, after 1 minute add the remaining shellfish. Turn every 30 seconds until the prawns are cooked (the tiger prawns will be blue at first, as soon as they turn pink, it is cooked).

Being careful not to burn your hands, reassemble the kebabs and serve (please note the lemon grass stick is for decoration and to flavour the dish, not to eat on its own).

Main Courses

Cider battered haddock, 'tartared' peas and chips
Mackerel, bruschetta, asparagus and apple with fennel sauce
Paella
Gurnard, pickled beetroot and cannelloni
Crispy Calamari with lime dipping sauce and hot and sour dipping sauce
Buttered cod, chicory and broccoli puree
BBQ monk fish, Jerusalem artichokes, baby spinach and sautéed potatoes
Sea bass in a herb crust, lemon rice, honey and mustard broccoli and spinach
Octopus and stuffed squid open pie
Roast brill, fried mushrooms, new potatoes and a spicy BBQ sauce
Trout in a pepper, melon and coconut sauce with samphire and fondant potatoes

Ham, chicken, mushroom and banana pizza with a barbecue base
Pork loin fillet with apple, butternut squash and broccoli
Lasagne
Peppered steak, green beans and sweet potato
Beef burger, cheddar and balsamic chutney, oven chips
Roulade of pork, orange sauce and sweet potato
Rack of lamb, plum sauce, mash potato and garlic carrots and baby sweetcorn

Chicken, spring onion and pak choi kebab with satay sauce
Caramelised duck, roasted dumplings, carrots and green leaf puree
Lime chicken, coconut rice and papaya salsa
Deep fried chicken strips with a lemon sauce and sweet and sour sauce
Roast Chicken, gingered leek, red cabbage and parsnips
Chicken dhansak with fragrant rice
Chicken Kiev, sweetcorn and muffin potatoes

Cider battered haddock with 'tartared' peas and chips (2 people)

You will need:

2 x 100g haddock fillets (skin on), 1 beaten egg, 1tsp French mustard, 30ml olive oil, juice of 1 lemon, 1tbs of chopped capers in vinegar, 100g frozen peas, 1 large potato, salt, 200ml cider, 3g dried yeast, 1tsp white wine vinegar, 250g plain flour plus extra for dusting, ½ tsp paprika, blue food dye, 2tsp fresh tarragon and extra for garnish

Prepare in advance:

The tartar: In a bowl add 1 beaten egg, 1tsp French mustard, 30ml olive oil, juice of 1 lemon, 1tbs chopped capers in vinegar and 2tsp finely chopped fresh tarragon. Add 100g frozen garden peas. Reserve for later.

The fish and batter: Add about 200ml cider, 3g dried yeast, ½ tsp salt, 1tsp white wine vinegar and up to 250g plain flour in a bowl and mix well; you want the batter to be very thick. Dust each haddock fillet in flour and then put into the batter and refrigerate for 1 hour.

The chips: Cut 1 potato into thick chips and add to 120°C deep fat fryer for 10 minutes. Drain and allow to cool.

Bring a pan of water to a simmer and get the deep fat fryer to 180°C. When at 180°C, add the fish to the oil.

Take the bowl with the tartar mixture and place it within the saucepan. The idea here is the steam from the simmering water cooks the tartar; however, the bowl should not touch the water so ensure you have used a suitably sized bowl which sits within the saucepan but doesn't fit inside! Allow the water to continue to gently simmer to very slowly cook the peas. Stir every 30 seconds or so until it becomes thick (about 10 minutes).

After the 10 minutes, remove the fish which should be nicely golden and put into the oven at 130°C to keep warm and add the chips to the fryer for about 5-10 minutes (until nicely browned).

Remember to keep stirring the tartar which should be thick now (turn the heat off the simmer and allow the residual heat to keep it warm).

Remove chips and coat in ½ tsp paprika and a pinch of salt.

To serve, simply place the fish in the middle with the chips on one side and the 'tartared' peas on the other. I also dye some rock salt blue (add a tiny drop to 1tsp of rock salt) and sprinkle this around the dish with a few sprigs of deep fried tarragon.

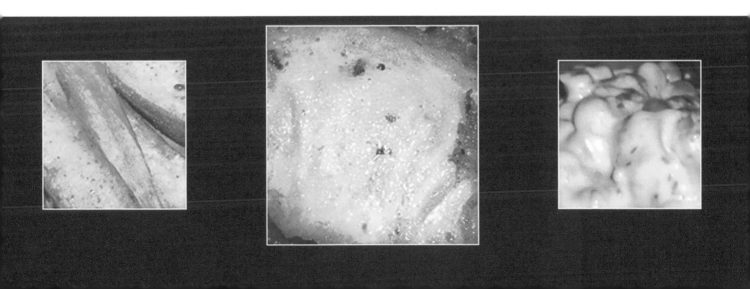

Mackerel, bruschetta, asparagus and apple with fennel sauce (2 people)

You will need:

2 mackerel fillets, flour, ½ tsp fennel seed, ½ fennel sliced into thin strips, 1 chopped and cored apple, half red onion, 20g butter, 2g fresh tarragon, 2 bruschetta slices, about 1 inch thick, 60ml extra virgin olive oil, 30ml white wine vinegar, 1tbs walnuts, 6 asparagus spears with bottoms removed, salt and pepper

Lightly flour both sides of each mackerel fillet and season with salt and pepper.

In a saucepan bring half a red onion (sliced into rings) to a low heat with 1tsp olive oil and add 1 roughly chopped and cored apple. Add ½ tsp fennel seed, ½ fennel (sliced into thin strips) and 20g butter and cook with lid on until onion is pink (about 30 minutes).

To make the vinaigrette add 1tbs chopped walnuts with 60ml extra virgin olive oil, 2g tarragon and 30ml white wine vinegar.

Toast the bruschetta slices.

Bring a pan of water to boil.

Bring a frying pan to heat and when hot add the fish skin side down. At the same time add 6 asparagus spears to the boiling water. Cook the asparagus for a total of 4 - 5 minutes. Cook the fish for about 2 -3 minutes, then turn them over, reduce heat and cook for 1 - 2 minutes.

Place the bruschetta on the plate, drizzle with the walnut vinaigrette, line the asparagus on top, place the fish on top and finally add the apple and fennel sauce to serve.

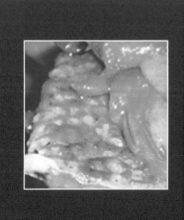
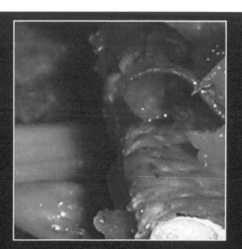

Paella (4 people)

You will need:

1 large squid with the head end removed (to create a hollow tube), 100g cod or haddock skinned and sliced into eight, 4 tiger prawns, shelled and ready (uncooked and blue), 50g cockles, 4 scallops, roe removed but kept for this dish, 1 lemon, 1 lime, 80g sushi rice, 25g spinach, 25ml full fat milk, a good pinch of saffron strands, 50ml white wine, 1-2tbs extra virgin olive oil, paprika

Add a good pinch of saffron to 25ml of full fat milk and leave for about 10 minutes.

Bring a pan of water to the boil, add 80g sushi rice and 25g spinach (make sure the water covers the rice). Reduce heat and simmer for 10 minutes.

After 10 minutes, drain the rice and reserve.

Bring a frying pan up to heat with 1tbs extra virgin olive oil.

Whilst waiting for the frying pan to get hot, return the rice to the saucepan and add the milk/saffron mixture and 50ml white wine. Turn to a low heat.

Add to the hot frying pan, in order, 4 tiger prawns, 5 seconds later 4 scallops, 5 seconds later 100g cod or haddock, 5 seconds later 4 roe from the scallops (if using) and 20 seconds later add 50g cockles. Cook until the prawns are almost fully pink (but still slightly under cooked; you can still see traces of the blue).

Add this fish mixture to the rice and gently cook on low with the juice of 1 lemon and a very small pinch of salt.

After 1 minute of the rice cooking, add the large squid to the frying pan with a little more oil and cook on all sides for about 2 minutes until well cooked and coloured.

To serve, slice the squid into quarters (and remove the tip so you have 4 hollow tubes) and stand up right on the plate. Spoon the paella mix into each squid ring. Lightly dust with paprika and serve with lime wedges.

Gurnard, pickled beetroot and cannelloni (4 people)

You will need:

8 fillets of gurnard, 200g sliced bacon, 80g kale, 150g La Buche (mild goats cheese), 125g mozzarella, 8 cannelloni tubes (shop bought is fine), 40g butter, 1tbs sifted plain flour, 4tbs milk, 1tbs rapeseed oil (aka canola), 4 bay leaves, 4 beetroots cut into 16 x 5mm discs, 100ml white wine vinegar, 2" cinnamon stick, 4 cloves, 2 black peppercorns, salt and black pepper

Prepare in advance:

Add to an air tight container 100ml white wine vinegar, 2" cinnamon stick, 4 cloves, 2 black peppercorns and 2 bay leaves and leave for 24 hours. After the 24 hour period remove the cinnamon and add 16 x 5mm beetroot discs and allow to pickle for another 24 hours.

In a frying pan, cook 200g sliced bacon and when half cooked, add 80g kale. When the kale has begun to wilt, turn off the heat and add 150g La Buche goats cheese and 125g mozzarella cheese. Allow to cool, stirring quite often to combine.

Put oven on to 180°C.

Boil 8 dried cannelloni tubes for 30 seconds. When cold, carefully stuff them with the bacon, kale and cheese mixture. Do this carefully and don't force too much in or the tubes will tear. Reserve any leftover mixture and sauce.

Add the cannelloni tubes to the oven and cook for approximately 20 minutes (or according to the packet instructions).

Add 2 bay leaves, a generous few twists of black pepper, 40g butter, 4tbs milk and 1tsp sifted plain flour to a saucepan. Heat until almost simmering then strain. Reserve liquid only and keep warm. This is the cheese sauce.

Lightly flour the fish with 2tsp plain flour and cook in 1tbs rapeseed oil on high heat for 2 − 3 minutes. Then turn and reduce the heat to low for 2 minutes.

When the cannelloni tubes are cooked, remove from oven and halve each tube (see picture below).

To serve, place 4 beetroot discs on each plate and stand each cannelloni on the disc. Place 2 fillets beside the 'towers' and drizzle over a small amount of the cheese sauce.

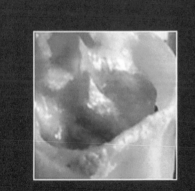
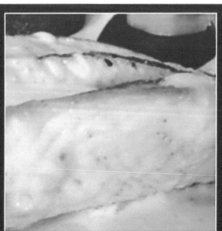

Crispy calamari with lime dipping sauce and hot and sour dipping sauce (2 people)

You will need:

8 baby squid, 2 eggs, 4tbs type OO flour, ½ tsp smoked paprika, 1tbs chopped ginger (keep peelings), 2 spring onions, 1tbs teriyaki sauce, 1 lime, 2tsp caster sugar, 1tbs Szechuan pepper corns, 2tbs sesame oil, 20ml red wine vinegar, 20ml Shaoxing wine, 20ml rice wine vinegar, 20ml black vinegar, 1½ tbs tomato ketchup, 1tsp cornflour, 1 finely chopped birds eye chilli, salt, pepper

Prepare in advance:

In a small saucepan, on a low heat infuse 1tbs Szechuan pepper corns with 2tbs sesame oil and 1 finely chopped bird's eye chilli. After 30 minutes, turn off heat and leave for 12 -24 hours. Drain and reserve the oil.

Empty, clean and washout the 8 baby squid (keeping tentacles). Slice into rings (I normally slice each squid into thirds). In a bowl, mix 2 eggs, 4tbs type OO flour, ½ tsp smoked paprika, a small pinch of salt and a little pepper to taste. Mix well until smooth. The mixture should be very thick. Add the squid rings and tentacles. Put into the fridge for an hour to cool.

To make the lime dipping sauce add 1tbs chopped ginger (with the peelings), 2 spring onions, 1tbs teriyaki sauce and the juice of lime to a saucepan. Bring to the boil for 30 seconds and then add 1tsp caster sugar and 50ml water and remove from heat. Leave for 20 minutes then strain and reserve liquid. Allow to cool.

To make the hot and sour sauce add 20ml red wine vinegar, 20ml Shaoxing wine, 20ml rice wine vinegar, 20ml black vinegar, 1tsp caster sugar and 1½ tbs tomato ketchup to the oil you created earlier. Bring to the boil.

Mix 1tsp cornflour with 2tbs water and add to the sauce. Turn off heat and stir. This will allow it to thicken. Keep warm.

Pre-heat your oven to 130°C.

Bring a deep fat fryer up to 180°C – 190°C and drop the squid rings into the fat one at a time. Don't over crowd your fryer as the temperature will drop. Each squid will take between 1 - 2 minutes to cook, but as soon as the batter has turned golden and crunchy, it is ready. Remove squid, drain on kitchen cloth and put into oven to keep warm and to drain further.

Serve with noodles or rice.

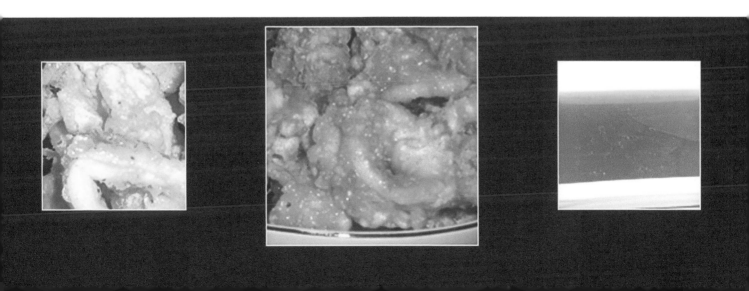

Buttered cod with chicory and broccoli puree (2 people)

You will need:

2 x 100g cod fillets, ½ broccoli, 1tsp caster sugar, 90ml double cream, 1 red chicory, 1tbs fresh oregano leaves, 1tbs plain flour, a knob of butter and salt.

Pat 2 x 100g cod fillets dry and very lightly sprinkle with 1tbs sieved plain flour and a small pinch of salt.

Bring a pan of water to the boil and cook the half a broccoli for 15 minutes.

After 10 minutes get a frying pan quite hot and add a knob of butter and the fish and cook until light and golden (or until you can see just over half of the fish is cooked). Then, turn heat to medium-low and flip fish over and add 1tbs oregano leaves.

Transfer broccoli to a blender (reserve boiling water and keep it boiling) and add 90ml double cream and 1tsp caster sugar to the broccoli; puree. Reserve the broccoli sauce and keep warm.

Add a dozen chicory leaves to the boiling water and blanche for about 1 minute. After this time, the fish should be fully cooked but check before serving.

Serving suggestion: Spoon the broccoli sauce onto a plate, place 6 chicory leaves horizontally in the middle and place the fish on top. Spoon any remaining melted butter over the fish.

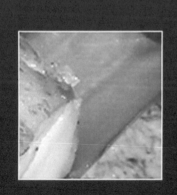

BBQ monk fish, Jerusalem artichokes, baby spinach and sautéed potatoes (4 people)

You will need:

2 x 125g monkfish, 1 red pepper, 2 limes, 4g fresh parsley, 4g fresh sage, 4g fresh oregano, 1 potato, 3 Jerusalem artichokes, 1tbs rapeseed oil (aka canola), a handful of pine nuts, a handful of spinach leaves

Prepare in advance:

Cook 1 red pepper in the oven at 200°C until blistered. Allow to cool. When cool, carefully remove the skin capturing all the juice which runs off. Half the pepper, discard all seeds and chop finely. In a large bowl, add the pepper (and juice), 2 juiced limes, the 2x 125g monkfish, 4g parsley, 4g sage and 4g oregano. Leave this to marinade and 'cook' for 6 hours (the lime juice will cook the fish)

Wash, peel and slice 1 potato into 5mm thick discs and 3 Jerusalem artichokes into 5mm slices.

Put the fish onto a medium heat barbecue trying to keep as much of the pepper from the marinade as possible on the fish.

Add potatoes and the artichokes to a frying pan with 1tbs rapeseed oil. Turn over potatoes and artichokes when the potatoes brown and add a handful of pine nuts. Turn fish over in barbecue (it's also really nice to add a bunch of herbs to the coals to allow the fish to cook in a herb smoke) and carefully baste with marinade juice (don't use too much of the liquid as this will make the coals cool, but it will make more smoke giving it a stronger BBQ taste).

When both side of potatoes are cooked and fish is hot throughout you can serve.

To serve, add the potato, artichoke, pine nuts (careful to not include too much oil) and a few spinach leaves randomly to each plate. Cut the monk fish into bit size pieces and place together in the middle.

Sea bass in a herb crust, lemon rice, honey and mustard broccoli and spinach (2 people)

You will need:

2 fillets of wild sea bass, 4tbs plain flour, 1 beaten egg, 3 slices of bread, 9g of mixed herbs (mix 3g basil, 4g parsley and 2g sage), 2 garlic cloves, 75g broccoli, 50g spinach, ½ tsp English mustard, 1 level tbs runny honey, juice of 1 lemon, 2tsp brandy, 1tbs olive oil, 80g long grain rice, 15g butter and salt.

Prepare in advance:

Create the bread crumb mix: In a food processor, blend 3 slices of bread, 3g basil, 4g parsley and 2g sage and 2 garlic cloves.

Create the lemon sauce for the rice: Add 10g butter, juice of 1 lemon and 2tsp brandy to a cup or measuring jug (no need to mix as this gets done later on).

Get 3 dinner sized plates out and add 4tbs plain flour with a pinch of salt to the first plate, 1 beaten egg to another and the bread crumb mix to the third.

Dust each bass fillet in flour, roll in beaten egg and then roll in bread crumb mix. Return to fridge for at least 20 minutes before continuing.

Boil 80g long grain rice (which will take 10 minutes) with enough water to cover by two inches. After 2 minutes, boil 75g broccoli in a separate saucepan (for a total time of 7 - 8 minutes).

After 2 minutes bring a frying pan to medium high heat with 1tbs olive oil. Add the fish and leave for about 4-6 minutes or until it's over half cooked (make sure you don't burn the bread crumb mixture). Turn the fish over and turn the heat down to low for another 3 - 4 minutes.

Add 50g spinach leaves to the broccoli for about 30 seconds. Drain, turn off heat and add 5g butter, 1 level tbs honey and ½ tsp English mustard and very gently stir.

Drain the rice, return to a low heat and add the lemon sauce. Keep stirring the rice for up to 1 minute – it should become 'gloopy' which will help you mould it for serving. At this point, it is ready.

Serve by placing the rice in the middle of plate in an oval shape, creating a well inside for the vegetable and place the fish on top.

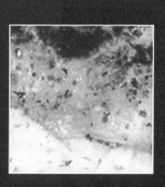

Octopus and stuffed squid open pie (2 people)

You will need:

125g octopus tentacles and arms, 6 baby squids (with tentacles), 170ml full fat milk, a pinch of saffron, 2 eggs, just over 130g type OO flour, 100g butter, 2 bay leaves, ½ red onion cut into rings, chopped fresh parsley, paprika, 40g diced chorizo, 30g diced black pudding, 1 finely chopped red mild red chilli, salt, 1tbs olive oil

Wash the squid and ensure their tubes are completely empty, reserving the tentacles.

Put oven onto 170°C.

In an electric mixer, blend 1 egg, 1 egg yolk, 130g type OO flour, 80g butter and a pinch of salt. Mix until it resembles bread crumbs and then roll out and line well buttered small pastry pins (or even a large muffin trays). Cook the pastry for 25 – 30 minutes (until golden).

During the pastry cooking time, add 40g dicedchorizo, 30g diced black pudding and the 1 mild finely chopped red chilli to a frying pan and cook until the chorizo is browned. Remove from heat. Be careful with the next bit so you don't burn your fingers.

When the mixture is cool enough to touch (however, the hotter the better) stuff this mixture evenly into the 6 baby squids. When all are full, roll each squid in a total of 1tbs flour and a pinch of salt.

Fry half a red onion (cut into rings) in the remaining oil from the chorizo and black pudding until soft. Add 2 bay leaves, a generous few twists of black pepper and 170ml full fat milk. Bring to a simmer and add a pinch of saffron, turn off heat and add 1tsp sifted type OO flour and 20g butter. Stir well until smooth and slightly thickened.

In a clean frying pan, add 1tbs of olive oil and fry the squid tentacles for 1 minute over a high heat, then add the 6 stuffed squids and 125g octopus. Fry for another 1½ minutes then turn everything over and fry for a further 1 minute. Turn off the heat and allow the residual heat to continue the cooking process.

To serve, place the pastry into the middle of the plate, place 3 squids inside the pastry, pour over a some of the red onion and saffron sauce, then the octopus and squid tentacles on top of the squid. Sprinkle over the top some chopped parsley and a light dusting of paprika powder.

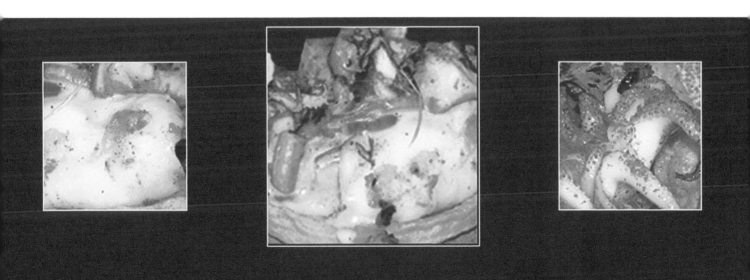

Roast brill, fried mushrooms, new potatoes and a spicy BBQ sauce (4 people)

You will need:

1 brill (approximately 2kg) scaled and filleted, 4 garlic cloves, 2 large vine tomatoes, 2 cherry tomatoes, 1 lemon, 1 red onion, 1 lime, 12 chestnut mushrooms, 4tbs white wine vinegar, 2tbs light muscovado sugar, 1tbs Worcestershire sauce, ½ tsp smoked paprika (add less if you don't want it spicy), 2tsp tomato ketchup, ¼ chicken stock cube, 20g butter, 3tbs chopped basil leaves, 5g chopped parsley, red wine vinegar, truffle oil, 3 bay leaves, 1tbs grated Parmesan cheese, 12-15 new potatoes, salt, pepper

Place the 2kg brill into a shallow oven proof dish and score. Add (gently scattered) 4 chopped garlic cloves, 2 diced large vine tomatoes, juice of ½ lemon with the other half cut into rings, 1 lime cut into rings, half red onion, cut into rings and 2tbs basil leaves.

Turn the oven on to 210°C.

In a saucepan add a finely chopped half red onion and sweat for 2 minutes in a small knob of butter. Add 4tbs white wine vinegar, 2tbs light muscovado sugar, 1tbs Worcestershire sauce, ½ tsp smoked paprika (add less if you don't want it spicy) and 2tsp tomato ketchup. Bring to a simmer and cook for 5 minutes then turn off heat. This can be re-warmed when required.

In a jug, create a stock by adding ¼ pint of water, ¼ of a chicken stock cube, 20g butter, 2tsp chopped basil and 5g chopped parsley.

Add the fish to the oven (it will take about 20 minutes to cook).

Bring a pan of water to boil and add 12 - 15 new potatoes and boil until just tender (between 15 - 25 minutes), then drain and add the stock. Cook until the sauce has disappeared.

In a medium heat frying pan, add 12 sliced chestnut mushrooms with a splash of red wine vinegar, a splash of truffle oil, 3 bay leaves and a tiny pinch of salt. Cook on medium heat for 3 minutes, and then add 1tbs Parmesan cheese, 2 chopped cherry tomatoes and ½ tsp basil leaves.

To serve, place the fish into the middle of the table and let people serve themselves.

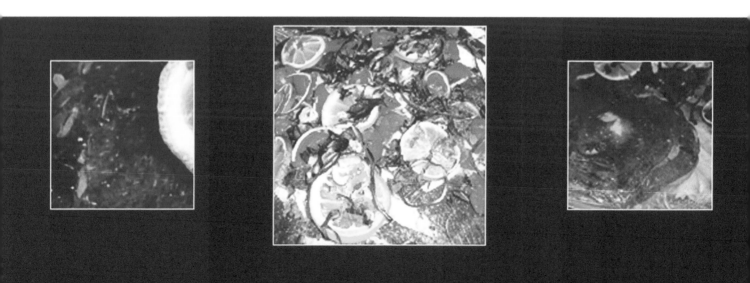

Trout in a pepper, melon and coconut sauce with samphire and fondant potatoes (2 people)

You will need:

1 red pepper, 100g honeydew melon flesh, 2 tsp coconut cream, 1 large potato, 2 fillets of trout, a handful of samphire, 1tbs rapeseed oil (aka canola), a little plain flour.

Blister 1 red pepper in a hot oven and allow to cool. Peel and discard the skin. Halve the pepper, remove all the pips and add the half pepper to a saucepan, with 100g chopped honeydew melon flesh and bring to a simmer. Blend the pepper/melon mixture until smooth. Add 1 ½ tsp coconut milk and keep this sauce warm.

Wash and peel the potato and cut into 3-4cm long cylinders (use an apple corer to shape) and brown in a frying pan with 1tbs rapeseed oil. When nicely browned, add ½ pint of chicken stock and boil. Keep testing the potato to see when it is ready. Approximately 10 minutes.

When the potatoes are 90% cooked, turn off the heat and bring a frying pan to heat with 1tbs rapeseed oil and add 2 fillets of lightly floured trout, skin down and allow to cook for 3-5 minutes, then turn over, turn heat down and cook for a further 2 − 3 minutes. During this time, bring a pan of water to boil and blanche a handful of samphire for 30 seconds − 1 minute.

To serve, I spoon 5 - 7 tablespoons of the sauce onto a plate, and add the fish into the middle. I surround it with fondant potatoes and samphire and drizzled up to 1tsp of coconut milk randomly into the sauce.

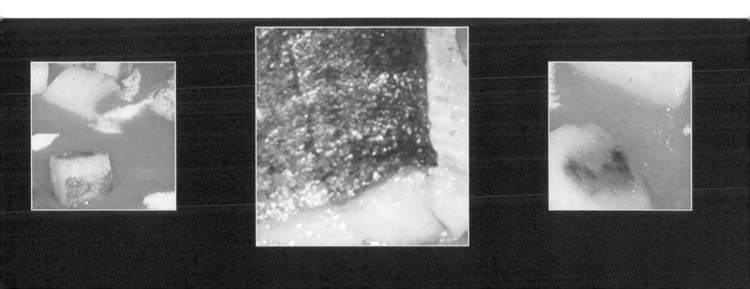

Ham, chicken, mushroom and banana pizza with a barbecue base (serves 2 - 3)

You will need:

170g type OO flour, 40g strong white bread flour, 4g dried yeast, 1 tsp sugar, ½ tsp sea salt, 2 tbs olive oil, 1 red onion, lots of fresh basil leaves basil (to taste), 4tbs white wine vinegar, 1tbs muscovado sugar, 1tbs Worcestershire, a dash of Tabasco sauce, 4tbs tomato puree, 100g mozzarella cheese. Optional toppings: 1 banana, a few mushrooms, some chicken breasts pieces, some ham, some oregano

Prepare in advance:

In a food processor, mix 170g type OO flour, 40g strong white bread flour, 4g dried yeast, 1 tsp sugar and ½ tsp sea salt with a hand full of basil leaves. Blend for 20 seconds. Then add 1½ tbs olive oil, start blending again and slowly add between 60-80ml of warm water until it just begins to form a large ball of dough which is slightly wet and sticky to the touch. Kneed by hand for a further 5 minutes on a well floured surface, then gently roll into a ball and leave it out in a bowl loosely covered with cling film. Do not leave this in fridge; it must remain at room temperature for about 20 – 30 minutes.

Create the barbecue base by chopping ½ red onion into small pieces and cooking until soft in a drop of olive oil. Add 4tbs white wine vinegar, 1tbs muscovado sugar, 1tbs Worcestershire, a dash of Tabasco sauce and bring to a simmer. As soon as it simmers, remove from heat and add 4tbs tomato puree and mix well.

Pre-heat oven to 220°C.

After the pizza has rested for about 30 minutes, gently roll the dough out into the shape and size, dust the underside with flour and place onto a very hot oiled stone pizza tray. Spread a good few spoonfuls of barbecue mix right to edges of the dough. Add 100g chopped mozzarella evenly to the pizza.

As for toppings, it really is up to you but I love a hand full of chicken, mushrooms, ham, the other half of the red onion (sliced in to rings), 1 chopped banana and a small handful of oregano leaves.

When your pizza is assembled, return it to the oven at 220°C and cook until the cheese has melted and just started to turn golden.

Pork loin fillet with apple, butternut squash and broccoli (2 people)

You will need:

½ butternut squash, 1 peeled and chopped potato, 1 peeled and chopped carrot, 2 x pork loins, 2tbs honey, a few chopped fresh sage leaves, 1 apple, juice of 1 lime, several broccoli florets, a knob of butter.

Set the oven to 200°C

Bring an oven proof pot of water to the boil and add ½ of a chopped butternut squash and 1 peeled and chopped potato and boil for 5 minutes, then add 1 peeled and chopped carrot and a few broccoli florets and boil for another 4 minutes. Drain.

On a high heat, add a knob of butter to the pot and cook the pork with only the fat touching the bottom of the pot. Cook until well crisped, then colour all sides of the pork. Remove pork and leave on the side

Add the butternut squash, potato, carrot and broccoli to the pot and cook in the oven for about 20 minutes (or until the vegetables have just started to colour).

Peel the apple and then slice into 6 rings and chop the remainder into cubes. Drizzle with lime juice.

After the 20 minutes is up, add 2tbs honey to the vegetables with the apple cubes, stir round and add the pork for a further 10 - 15 minutes (or until the pork is cooked). 5 minutes before the end, add the apple rings and sage to the dish.

To serve, I placed all the vegetables in a pile in the middle, sat the pork on top with 3 apple slices on top of the pork, slightly overlapping. Sprinkle over a few sage leaves.

Lasagne (8 people)

You will need:

300ml full fat milk, 8 cracked black pepper corns, 2 bay leaves, ½ crushed nutmeg, 90g butter, 18g plain flour (sifted), 350g type OO flour, 2 large eggs, 100g spinach, 1 chopped leek, 50ml red wine, 800g tinned tomatoes, 200g tomato puree, 1tbs caster sugar, 2 red onions, 8 garlic cloves, 4 chestnut mushrooms, 250g mascarpone, a handful of grated cheddar cheese, a handful of grated red Leicester cheese, 3 chopped bacon rashers, a handful of basil leaves, 500g mince beef.

Prepare in advance:

The béchamel sauce: Add 300ml full fat milk into a pan with the 8 cracked black pepper corns, 1 chopped leek, 2 torn bay leaves and ½ crushed nutmeg. Allow to infuse on lowest heat for 30 minutes. If the milk begins to simmer, remove from heat and return again a minute later. Keep spooning off any skin that forms. After 30 minutes strain and discard all solids. Add 40g butter and 18g sifted flour and mix until very smooth and creamy using an electric hand whisk or blender. When smooth, add 250g mascarpone.

The tomato sauce: In a food processor, blend 800g tinned tomatoes, 200g tomato puree, 1tbs caster sugar, 2 red onions, 8 garlic cloves and 4 chestnut mushrooms.

In a saucepan, add a knob of butter (50g), mince beef (500g) and 3 chopped bacon rashers and brown for 5 minutes then add the tomato sauce and 50ml red wine and cook for approximately 1 hour on low with the lid half off.

Wilt 100g spinach leaves and drain (squeeze out any liquid) and blend until smooth. Add to 350g type OO flour and 2 large beaten eggs and kneed (adding more flour or a little water if too dry of wet) until homogenous. Use a pasta maker (or a rolling pin) to shape into pasta sheets.

In an oiled lasagne sized dish, alternate lasagne sheets, meat and then béchamel sauce until dish is full, ending with meat. I normally use 4 or 5 layers of the lasagne sheets. On top, put a hand full of grated cheddar, a handful of red Leicester cheese and half a handful of basil leaves. Cook in 180°C for 30 - 45 minutes, or until golden. Sprinkle with the remaining basil leaves.

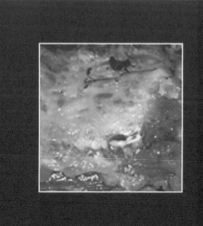
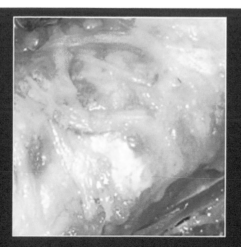

Peppered steak, green beans and sweet potato (2 people)

You will need:

6g black peppercorns, 2 x 200g sirloin steak, 1tsp English mustard, 180g julienned sweet potatoes, 60g julienned green beans, 2 chopped garlic cloves, 20g butter, 2tsp rapeseed oil (aka canola), 1tbs flammable rum, 2tbs double cream, salt

Prepare in advance:

In a pestle and mortar crush the 6g black peppercorns. Rub ¼ tsp of English mustard into each side of the steak and press each side of the steak into a quarter of the crushed peppercorns. Refrigerate for 20 minutes.

Add 180g julienned sweet potatoes, 60g green beans, 2 chopped garlic cloves and 10g butter to a frying pan and sauté.

After 5 minutes add 2tsp of rapeseed oil to another frying pan and add the steak when the pan is hot. Turn when half way cooked to your liking and add 1tbs rum. Set the rum alight and allow the steak to flambé. When the flames have died, add 2tbs double cream and 10g butter. By the time the steak is cooked, the vegetables should also be nicely cooked.

Serve. Place the steak on one side of a rectangle shaped plate and the sweet potato green bean mixture on the other. Spoon the cream sauce generously over the steak.

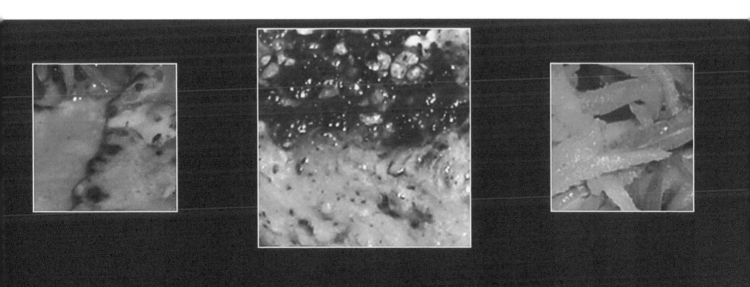

Beef burger, cheddar and balsamic chutney, oven chips (4 people)

You will need:

400g mince beef, 2 beaten eggs, 4 garlic cloves, 8g mixed herbs (2g fresh oregano, 2g fresh parsley, 2g fresh basil, 2g fresh sage), 2tsp Worcestershire sauce, ½ red onion, 1tbs English mustard, 1tbs red wine vinegar, 1tbs rapeseed oil, 2 fresh bay leaves, 80g chopped cheddar cheese, ½ white onion, 40ml balsamic vinegar, Tabasco sauce, 2-3tbs olive oil, 4 quartered cherry tomatoes, 250g red mozart potatoes, 1tbs plain flour, 1tsp dried oregano, 4 burger buns.

Prepare in advance:

Burgers: In a bowl, mix 2 beaten eggs, 4 roughly chopped garlic cloves, 8g mixed herbs, ½ finely chopped red onion, 2tsp Worcestershire sauce, 1tbs English mustard, a dash of Tabasco sauce, 1tsp olive oil and 400g mince beef. Using a chef ring, shape into burgers (approximately 200g each). Refrigerate for about an hour.

Pre-heat oven to 180°C.

Wash (do not peel) 250g red mozart potatoes. Cut into chips and boil for 3 minutes in water. Add to an oven proof dish and add 1½ tbs olive oil and mix well. Sprinkle over 1tbs plain flour. Cook for about 25 minutes.

After 10 minutes, bring a frying pan to a medium-high heat and add 2 cracked bay leaves, 1tbs red wine vinegar and 1tbs rapeseed oil.

Add the burgers and brown on each side, about 4 minutes per side.

Transfer to oven 10 - 15 minutes (until cooked).

Add ½ roughly chopped white onion and 4 quartered cherry tomatoes to a saucepan on medium heat with 2tsp olive oil and cook until soft. Add 40ml balsamic vinegar and turn off the heat. Add 80g chopped cheddar cheese. The aim is to allow the cheddar to only just melt.

When the chips are finished, toss in 1tsp dried oregano. Place the burger buns in the oven for 1 minute.

Open up a burger bap, put the burger on and add the lettuce and then spoon the cheese sauce over. Serve with the oven chips.

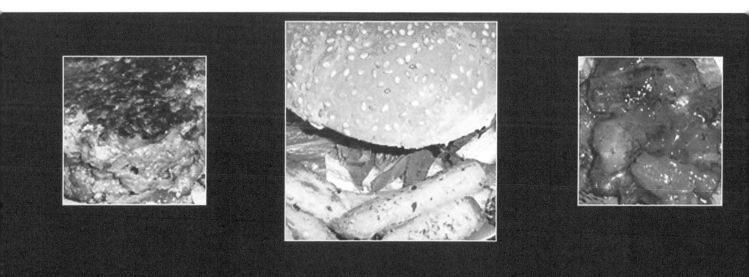

Roulade of pork, orange sauce and sweet potato (2 people)

You will need:

4tsp walnut oil, 2 chopped shallots, 2tbs southern comfort, 40g spinach leaves, a knob of butter, 5tsp fresh thyme leaves, 1 sweet potato, ½ tsp sugar, 100ml orange juice, 8 juniper berries, 2 pork loins, 4g fresh chopped parsley.

In a saucepan, cook 2 chopped shallots in 2tsp walnut oil until soft then add 2tbs of southern comfort. Turn off heat and add 40g spinach leaves, a knob of butter and 1tsp fresh thyme leaves. Leave until cool then empty the saucepan, reserving contents.

Add 100ml water and ½ tsp sugar to the saucepan and bring to boil. When boiling add 100ml orange juice and reduce to medium-low heat. Add 8 juniper berries and burst each. When the sauce has been reduced by half allow to cool and reserve liquid and discard berries.

Put oven onto 180°C.

Place each pork loin on a chopping board, cover in foil and using a rolling pin, gently roll the pork out so it's about 1/3 longer than it was originally. Combine the orange sauce with the shallots, stir and leave for 10 minutes. After 10 minutes, add 1 - 2tsp of the onion from this sauce into the middle of the pork (you will also 'capture' the other flavours as well, which is fine). Roll the pork up like a swiss roll. Using a wooden tooth pick, carefully spear the meat to ensure it holds its shape. Repeat for the other pork loin.

Place in the oven for about 20 – 30 minutes (until cooked to your liking).

Wash, peel and very finely slice 1 sweet potato length ways for long thin strips. Add to boiling water for 2 minutes and drain. Add the boiled sweet potato to a frying pan and cook on high heat with 2tsp walnut oil.

In a saucepan bring the remainder of the orange sauce to the boil and add 5tsp fresh thyme leaves and 4g fresh chopped parsley leaves.

To serve, place the crispy sweet potato on the plate and rest the pork on top. Drizzle the sauce around the meat and plate.

Rack of lamb (2 people)

You will need:

2 whole plums, 1tsp caster sugar, 1 stick of cinnamon, 2 x 300g rack of lambs, 2 peeled and chopped potatoes, 6 baby carrots, 6 baby corn, 15g butter, 1 sprig of rosemary

In a saucepan, add 2 whole plums, 1tbs water, 1tsp caster sugar, 1 whole stick cinnamon and slowly cook for about 30 minutes with lid on, stirring occasionally. When the plums break up, you can remove the stones.

Bring a large of pan of water to the boil and preheat the oven to 180°C.

Par boil 6 baby carrots for 6 minutes and 6 baby corn for 3 minutes then transfer to a plate (keep the water from the pan).

Cut the fat off both the lamb racks and place it back on top of the lamb. Cook the lamb in the oven for approximately 25 minutes at 180°C then leave to rest for 2 minutes. The lamb fat is on top so as it cooks, the fat drips onto the meat.

During this cooking time, add 2 peeled and well chopped potatoes to the pan of water and boil for about 25 minutes with 1 sprig of rosemary.

5 minutes before the end of the lamb's cooking time, add 15g butter to a frying pan and fry the carrot and baby corn through until nicely coloured.

Drain the potatoes, remove the rosemary and add a knob of butter and with salt and pepper and mash until creamy.

To serve, I use a chef ring to make a ring of mash potato in the middle of the plate and around this I place the carrots and baby corn, overlapping each other and alternating. Carefully place the lamb on the mash and add 1 - 2tbs of the plum sauce.

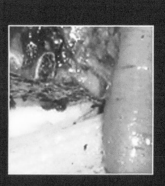

Chicken, spring onion and pak choi kebab with satay sauce (2 people)

You will need:

2tsp ground nut oil, ½ small finely chopped white onion, 150ml coconut milk, 2tbs light soy sauce, 2tbs crunchy peanut butter, 1 finely chopped chilli, 1 chopped garlic clove, 2tsp finely chopped fresh ginger, 1 tsp ground coriander, ¼ tsp turmeric, 1tbs runny honey, 1 pak choi broken into the individual leaves, 1 spring onion and 2 chopped chicken breasts (chop large enough to fit on kebab skewers), 2 wooden kebab skewers

Prepare in advance:

Chicken marinade: 1 chopped garlic clove, 2tsp finely chopped ginger, 1tsp ground coriander, ¼ tsp turmeric, 1tbs light soy sauce and 1tbs runny honey to two chopped chicken breasts.

Preheat oven to 180°C.

On a medium heat add 2tsp ground nut oil with ½ finely chopped white onion to a saucepan and cook until the onion is soft. Add 150ml coconut milk, 1tbs light soy, 2tbs peanut butter and 1 finely chopped chilli. Stir until well mixed and creamy. Reduce heat to low.

Skewer the chicken with a wooden kebab stick in the following order: pak choi leaf, chicken, a slice of spring onion, chicken (continue until kebab stick is full). Repeat for other kebab stick. Cook the kebabs for 10 minutes in the oven.

Spoon away any excess oil from the satay sauce.

Serve with jasmine rice.

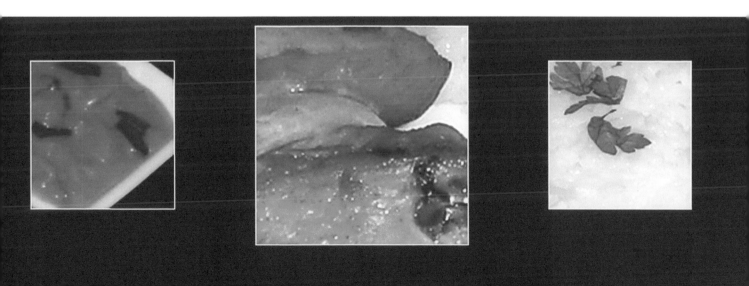

Caramelised duck, roasted dumplings, carrots and green leaf puree (serves 4)

You will need:

4 duck breasts, 2 potatoes, 80g plain flour, 40g vegetable suet, 2 julienned carrots, 50g mixture of spinach, rocket and watercress, 60ml double cream, salt, 2 chopped garlic cloves, 15g butter, 16 fresh sage leaves, 1 pear, pepper, half chicken stock cube, 1tbs sunflower oil, 1 tsp caster sugar, 2 tsp olive oil

Prepare in advance:

Garlic carrots: Julienne 2 washed and peeled carrots. Leave aside with 15g of butter and 2 chopped garlic cloves.

Dumplings: Wash, peel quarter and core 1 pear. Finely dice one quarter. Mash one quarter (to create a pear paste). Reserve the remaining half. In a mixing bowl, mix 80g plain flour, 40g vegetable suet, 10 roughly chopped sage leaves, a pinch of salt and some of the pear pieces. Mix by hand until dough like. Add pear paste! Roll out until about 3-5mm thick, and cut into 4 rectangle strips.

Bring a pan of water to boil with half a chicken stock cube and a pinch of salt. Reduce to a simmer, and add the rectangular dumplings. Cook for approximately 10-15 minutes. Remove dumplings from water (reserve water) and leave on side.

Wash 2 peeled potatoes and cut into discs about 4mm in thickness and add to the simmering water and simmer for about 5 minutes. Drain and add potatoes to a frying pan (the frying pan needs to be cold; the potato is just going to 'rest' here) with 1tbs sunflower oil.

Pre-heat oven to 200°C. Bring the frying pan with potatoes in up to a high heat and sauté for approximately 8 minutes. During these 8 minutes, bring up the heat in the second pan (to high) with 1tsp olive oil. When the oil is hot, add the duck breasts skin down! Add the finely diced pear quarters to the pan with the duck. Put dumplings into oven on an oven rack. Cook duck for 8 minutes (do not turn over).

[continues on next page]

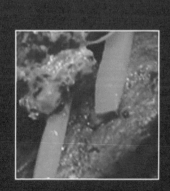
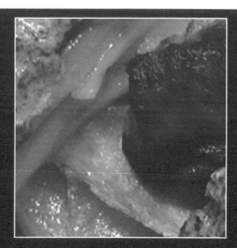

After 8 minutes, tip duck oil/juice over potatoes. Then turn duck over, cook on other side for 2 minutes. Turn potatoes over, turn both frying pan heats to medium (check on dumplings – turn if needed).

After 2 minutes, remove duck, slice off fat from the duck and then slice duck breast into strips. The strips should be pink and under cooked. Return everything to frying pan (including skin) and toss.

In an empty saucepan add 50g mix of watercress, spinach and rocket (these can be bought already made up) with 1tsp sugar, 1tsp olive oil and 60ml double cream. Remove all stalks from salad, and blend until smooth with a hand blender. Turn off heat.

When the duck is almost cooked, move the duck to edge of frying pan and add carrots, garlic and butter to the pan. Turn heat off potatoes and duck (residual heat will continue to cook everything) and serve. I placed 4 sautéed potatoes in a line, rested the roasted dumpling on top and alternated a few duck pieces, green leaf puree, carrot, duck, carrot, green leaf puree, duck.

Lime chicken with coconut rice and a papaya salsa (2 people)

You will need:

2 chicken breasts, 2tbs teriyaki sauce, 2tbs lime marmalade, 2tsp toasted sesame oil, ½ tsp sugar, 1 papaya, 2 large spring onions, 2 tomatoes, ½ deseeded birds eye chilli, 2 limes, 1 lemon, 70g long grain rice, 50ml creamed coconut, a few fresh chopped coriander, 1tbs ground nut oil

Prepare in advance:

Add the juice of 1 lime, 2tbs teriyaki sauce, 2tbs lime marmalade, 1tsp toasted sesame oil, 2 chicken breasts sliced into strips and ½ tsp sugar. Leave to marinade 30 minutes.

Prepare the Salsa 20 minutes before ready to cook and do not refrigerate. To a large bowl add 1 papaya, diced (remove pips), juice of 1 lime, juice of 1 lemon, 1tsp toasted sesame oil, 2 large spring onions sliced length ways, 2 diced tomatoes, ½ birds eye chilli chopped very finely.

Add 70g long grain rice to boiling water and cook for 12 minutes so the rice is well cooked.

About half way through the rice cooking, bring a griddle pan up to heat with 1tbs of ground nut oil. Add the chicken but reserve most of the marinade.

When the pink uncooked chicken is no longer visible (so it's still slightly under cooked), add the remainder of the marinade and continue to cook, stirring quite often. Be careful, you want the sugars in the marmalade to caramelise but not burn so keep a close eye on it.

When the rice is cooked, drain the rice and then return the rice to the pan (off the heat). Add the chopped coriander and 50ml creamed coconut. Mix until rice becomes 'gloopy' (this should be only a few seconds).

To serve, I use a square chef ring and add the rice. The coconut which made it 'gloopy' will help to keep its shape. I gently spoon the chicken on top of the rice and add a handful of salsa (drain salsa first).

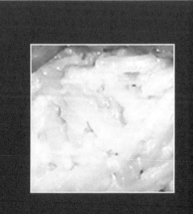
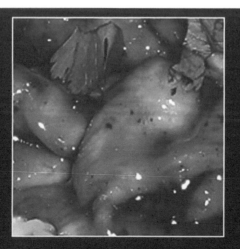

Deep fried chicken strips with a lemon sauce and sweet and sour sauce (2 people)

You will need:

2 chicken breasts, 2 ½ lemons, 3tbs Chinese rice vinegar, 1tsp sesame oil, 1tsp Teriyaki sauce, 1 broken lemon grass stick, 3tbs sugar, 1tsp soy sauce, 2tsp cornstarch, 20ml red wine vinegar, 20ml Shaoxing wine, 1tbs tomato ketchup, 20ml pineapple juice, 2 eggs, 1 egg yolk, 5tbs plain flour, a few coriander leaves, 1 finely chopped garlic clove, 2g chopped ginger

Prepare in advance:

Slice the 2 chicken breasts into strips, cutting along the width of the chicken breast. Finely chop a few coriander leaves, 1 garlic clove and 2g ginger. Mix together. Make a small incision in each chicken breast and stuff with a little of this mixture.

In a small bowl, mix 2 eggs and 1 egg yolk with 5tbs plain flour and 1tsp Teriyaki sauce. Mix well and add the chicken. Refrigerate for 1 hour.

Make the corn starch paste by mixing 1tsp cornstarch with 1tbs water.

To make the lemon sauce, add the juice of 2 lemons into a saucepan with 1tbs Chinese rice vinegar and 1tsp sesame oil and bring to a boil. As soon as it starts to boil add the corn starch paste and then reduce heat to medium low and add 1 broken lemon grass stick, 1tbs sugar and 1tsp soy sauce. After one minute, add 170ml water. Remove the lemon grass and keep the sauce warm.

To make the sweet and sour sauce add 20ml red wine vinegar to a saucepan with 20ml Shaoxing wine, 1tbs tomato ketchup, 2tbs sugar, 20ml pineapple juice, juice of half a lemon and 2tbs Chinese rice vinegar. Bring to the boil.

Make the corn starch paste by mixing 1tsp cornstarch with 1tbs water. Add this to the pan and stir well.

Reduce the heat of the pan to low, add 20ml water and keep warm.

Bring an oven to 130°C.

Bring a deep fat fryer to 180°C (with the oil already in) and drop the chicken strips in being careful not to add to many at once or the temperature will drop. Cook each batch for about 5 minutes then transfer to the oven to keep warm.

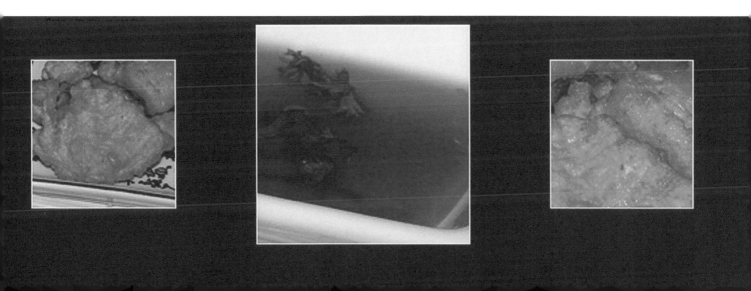

Roast chicken breasts, gingered leek, parsnips and red cabbage (2 people)

You will need:

2 chicken breasts, 1 small red cabbage (100g), 1 large peeled parsnip cut lengthways into eights, 10g finely chopped ginger, 1 leek cut into strips (lengthways), 2 fresh bay leaves, 1 diced and cored apple, 1tbs red wine vinegar, 2tsp honey, 1tsp dried oregano, salt and pepper, 20g Parmesan cheese, 6 Parma ham slices, 15g butter, 1tbs olive oil

Prepare in advance:

Chicken stuffing: Melt 20g Parmesan cheese with 15g butter. Add 1tsp dried oregano leaves and stir. Allow to cool. Divide into two portions. Make a slice in the top of the chicken all the way down the breast and push the melted Parmesan mixture into the chicken breast with any remaining butter.

Cut the parsnip into eight (lengthways) and then par boil for 5 minutes.

Slice 100g red cabbage into strips and add in a pan with 1tbs red wine vinegar, 2 tsp water, 2 fresh bay leaves and 1 diced and cored apple. Cook on a low heat for 45 minutes with lid on. Take the lid off for last 5 minutes.

During this cooking time, pre-heat oven to 180°C.

Blanche the sliced leek for 2 minutes in boiling water, then add to a frying pan with 10g ginger, 1tbs olive oil and a few twists of black pepper (the frying pan should not be on).

Add the parsnips to the oven for about 30 minutes with 2tsp honey and 1tsp dried oregano.

At the same time, add the chicken to the oven and after 20 minutes, remove the chicken from the oven and wrap each breast in 3 slices of Parma ham (be careful, the chicken should be quite hot).

Turn the heat on the leeks (stir often but allow it to colour) and return the chicken to the oven for 10 minutes.

To serve, place a pile of straight leeks on the plate, rest the chicken on top and add parsnip and red cabbage either side, removing the bay leaves from the cabbage.

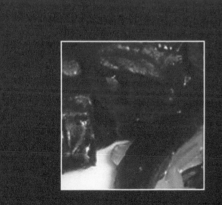
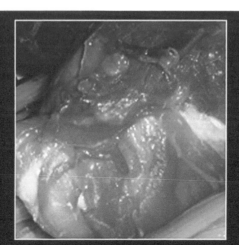
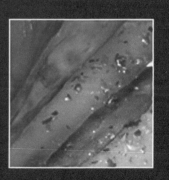

Chicken dhansak with fragrant rice (2 people)

You will need:

3 garlic cloves, 10g chopped ginger, ¼ tsp coriander powder, ½ tsp cumin powder, ¼ tsp fennel seed, ¾ tsp cinnamon powder, 2 fresh green birds eye chillies (or 1 if you prefer mild), ½ tsp fenugreek powder, ½ tsp mustard seeds, 2 cardamon pods, 2 chicken breasts, ½ white onion, 2tbs groundnut oil, ¼ tsp turmeric powder, ½ tsp garam masala powder, 80g red lentils, 200g diced sweet potato, 150g diced butternut squash, 1tbs sugar, 1tbs tamarind paste, 25ml full fat yoghurt, 80g basmati rice, 1tbs milk, 10g butter, ¼ tsp caraway seeds, 2 cloves, salt and pepper

Prepare in advance:

In a food processor, blend 3 garlic cloves, 10g chopped ginger, ¼ tsp coriander powder, ½ tsp cumin powder, ¼ tsp fennel seed, ½ tsp cinnamon powder (you use the other ¼ for the rice), 2 fresh birds eye chilli (or one for mild) with stalk removed, several twists of black pepper, ½ tsp fenugreek powder, ½ tsp mustard seeds and ¼ tsp salt until fairly smooth (no lumps!). Transfer this to a bowl, add 2 cracked open cardamon pods, 6tbs water and marinade 2 chopped chicken breasts for 4 hours.

Sieve and wash 80g basmati rice until water runs clear and then leave in a jug of cold water.

Bring a pan of water to boil and add 200g diced sweet potato and 150g diced butternut squash and boil for 5 minutes, then drain.

Heat ½ chopped white onion in 2tbs ground nut oil until very soft. Add ¼ tsp turmeric powder and ½ tsp garam masala. Turn heat to high and when hot add the chicken (with some of the marinade) and lightly brown the chicken. Turn heat down to medium high and add 80g red lentils and cook for 2 minutes with lid on. Stir half way through. Add the sweet potato and butternut squash and cook for another 5 minutes (stir often), turn the heat to medium low heat and add 270g water and cook with lid on for 15 minutes. During this time, bring a pan of water to boil for rice. Stir the chicken often.

Pre-heat oven to 170°C.

After the 15 minutes is up, take lid off, turn heat to medium high and cook for 10 more minutes, add 1tbs sugar and 2 – 3 tsp tamarind paste (to taste) and the remainder of the marinade. Turn heat back down to medium. Drain the rice from the cold water and add rice to the boiling water and cook for 8 - 10 minutes (until rice is soft).

Whilst the rice is cooking, prepare in a small cup 1tbs milk, 10g butter, ¼ tsp caraway seed, ¼ tsp cinnamon powder and 2 cloves. When the rice is cooked, transfer to an oven proof dish and add this sauce and mix well. Cook in oven for 10 minutes. By this time, the dhansak should be nice and thick. Add 25ml yoghurt to the dhansak, mix well and serve.

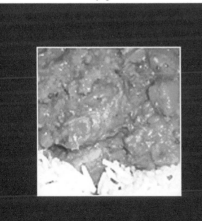

Chicken Kiev, sweetcorn and muffin potatoes (2 people)

You will need:

6 garlic cloves, 7g fresh basil, 3g fresh parsley, 60g butter, 2 chicken breasts, 1 large potato, 4 slices of 1 day old white bread (slightly stale is good), 2tbs flour, 3 beaten eggs, 2 corn on the cobs, 1 sprig of fresh rosemary, 100g Philadelphia cheese

Prepare in advance:

Finely chop 6 garlic cloves, 7g basil and 3g parsley. Add 50g butter and melt until soft and malleable.

Slit open both chicken breasts from the side (the width is wider than the height so by doing at the side we can fit more filling in). Spoon as much garlic butter as you can into each chicken and then transfer to the fridge until set. Reserve any remaining garlic butter.

In a food processor add the remaining garlic butter with 4 de-crusted slightly stale white bread slices and blitz until you have bread crumbs remaining.

When the chicken breasts are cold and the garlic butter inside has set inside, put a plate out and add 2tbs flour; coat both the breasts evenly and then dip into 2 beaten eggs. Finally, coat in the bread crumb mixture and return to the fridge for 1 hour.

Bring a pan of water to the boil and add 1 large finely chopped potato and boil for 20 minutes.

Heat the oven to 200°C and pre-heat a muffin tray.

Chop 2 sweetcorn cobs into quarters and put into tin foil and wrap up with a 10g of butter, salt and pepper and a sprig of rosemary.

In a food processor, add 1 beaten egg, 100g Philadelphia, a pinch of salt, lots of black pepper, a knob of butter and the potato and blitz until creamy.

Get the muffin tray out of the oven and add a good drop of oil into each container (and grease around the sides) and fill each with the potato mixture and return to the oven.

5 minutes later, add the sweetcorn cobs into the oven. 15 minutes later, add the chicken on a different shelf for about 15 minutes (or until the chicken is cooked).

Serve on warm plates with the chicken in the middle and the muffin potatoes and sweetcorn cobs evenly placed around the plate.

Desserts

Amarasu

Flambé banana with brandy caramel

Ginger and mint cheese cake

Peach and chocolate mousse in chocolate cups

White chocolate parcels with berries, thyme and mint

Strawberry and vanilla cheese cake

Mango and toffee meringues

Hazelnut and honey parfait, rose jellies and vanilla caramels

Amarasu (8 people)

You will need:

80ml Amaretto (almond liqueur), 80ml Baileys, 24 sponge fingers, 100g type 00 flour, 100g butter, 4 eggs, 250g mascarpone, grated milk chocolate, 50g white caster sugar

In 2 batches, soak the 24 sponge fingers lightly in a 80ml Amaretto, 80ml baileys and 40ml water. The fingers need to soften only half of the way through, any more and they'll lose their texture and be too boozy!

Make the base by mixing 100g type 00 flour, 100g butter, 100g sugar, 2 eggs. Add 1tbs of this mix to the bottom of a greased dish and cook in the oven at 170°C until lightly brown (approximately 15 minutes). When cooked, remove with a spatula and place the biscuit on top of a wine bottle so the sides of the biscuit fall down. This will help shape the biscuit into a very subtle bowl shape. Be careful not to burn yourself as you may need to gently press down on the sides of the biscuit to help them shape. Be careful not to tear the biscuit. Repeat this 8 times.

Whisk 2 egg whites with 50g caster sugar until stiff and can forms peaks (as if making meringues).

In another bowl, add 2 egg yolks beat well until creamy. Gently add the 250g mascarpone to the egg yolk, and then gently fold the egg whites in.

Place the biscuit on a plate, add 3 halved sponge fingers (so, a total of 1 ½ fingers), add a spoonful of the cream mix, then another 3 halved sponge fingers on top of the cream and finally more cream mix to the top (building like a lasagne). Grate over milk chocolate to serve.

Flambé banana with brandy caramel (2 people)

You will need:

2 bananas sliced in half length ways, 1tbs sugar, 1 shot of brandy, 1 shot of dark rum, 2tbs medium maple syrup, 10g butter

Add 1tbs sugar with 1tsp water to a frying pan and bring to heat and as soon as it starts to caramelise (turn brown) add 1 shot of brandy, remove from heat and add 2tbs medium maple syrup and stir well.

Heat 10g butter in another frying pan, and as soon as it seems to be turning brown, add 2 sliced bananas, cook for 30 seconds and then add 1 shot of dark rum and set on fire. When the flame goes out, the banana is ready.

To serve, simply place the 2 bananas on the pate so the ends are touching and generously spoon over the brandy caramel.

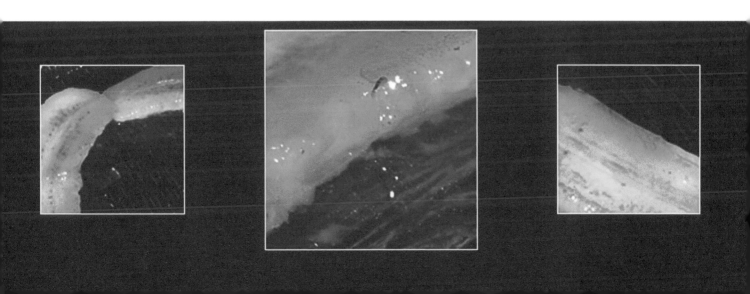

Ginger and mint cheese cake (4 people)

You will need:

4 ramekin glasses, 1 egg yolk, 200g Philadelphia cream cheese, 2tbs crème fraiche, 60g ginger in syrup, 2tbs sugar, 4g fresh mint leaves, 20g butter, 75g crumbled digestive biscuits, 1 gelatine leaf, grated milk chocolate as a garnish.

Soak the gelatine leaf for 5 minutes in cold water.

In a saucepan, on a low heat, add 200g Philadelphia cream cheese, 2tbs sugar and 2tbs crème fraiche and heat until melted. Add 1 egg yolk, 4g chopped mint leaves and 60g chopped ginger in syrup. Mix well.

Add the gelatine to the saucepan with the cheese sauce in and stir until absorbed. Remove from the heat.

Melt 20g butter and add 75g crumbled digestive biscuits (the easiest way is to wrap them in tin foil or a plastic bag and roll them with a rolling pin until crumbled) and mix to evenly coat.

Add 2tsp of the bread crumb mixture to the bottom of each ramekin glass and press down until even. Add the 'cheese' evenly to all 4 ramekins. Grate over milk chocolate when serving.

Peach and chocolate mousse in chocolate cups (8 people)

You will need:

300ml whipping cream, 1 egg, 2tbs caster sugar, 3tbs flaked almonds, 150g milk cooking chocolate, 120g white cooking chocolate, 70g dark cooking chocolate, 1 peach, 60ml amaretto liqueur, 8 washed balloons

Prepare in advance:

Slice 1 peach (leave skin on) into 16ths and soak in 60ml amaretto liqueur for 2 hours.

Add 100ml whipping cream to a pan and add 1 egg yolk (reserve white), 2 level tbs caster sugar and 3tbs flaked almonds. Mix well and bring to almost simmering for 2 minutes, stirring regularly. Remove from heat, add 150g milk chocolate and allow it to melt.

Whip 1 egg white until it forms peaks, and add to 200ml whipped whipping cream. Gently fold this into the chocolate mixture to complete the mousse.

Melt 120g white chocolate in a bowl.

In a separate bowl, melt 70g dark chocolate.

Blow up a balloon to a small bulb shape (smaller than your fist) and tie a knot. Dip it into the white chocolate so half is covered and place into a muffin tin, with the chocolate facing up. Do this for all the cups you want to make and refrigerate. Then, after 30 minutes, repeat with more white chocolate. After another 30 minutes in the fridge, repeat with dark chocolate but only do this once. After another 30 minutes, carefully burst each balloon and slowly remove the balloon from the chocolate cup without letting the chocolate melt (this takes practice); you are left with the chocolate cups. Depending on how thick you like your cups, you may have to add more melted chocolate.

Fill each chocolate cup up with the chocolate mousse (ensuring you get some of the almonds) and place 2-3 peach slices on top.

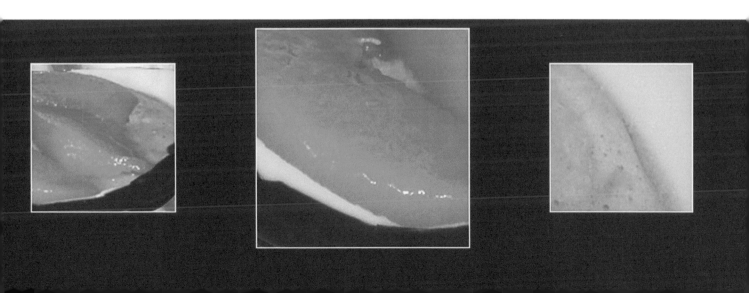

White chocolate parcels (4 people)

You will need:

4tbs single cream, 1 vanilla pod, 150g white cooking chocolate, 1 gelatine sheet, 1 egg, 50g type OO flour, 50g caster sugar, 50g butter, 2 strawberries, 4 blackberries, ½ tsp mint and literally just a few thyme leaves

Pre-heat oven to 170°C.

Make the biscuit batter by melting 50g butter and then adding 50g type OO flour, 50g caster sugar and 1 egg and mix until very smooth.

Add 1tbs at a time of the biscuit batter to a greased baking tray and cook for about 10 minutes (or until the edges are slightly brown and the centre golden).

Shape the biscuits while hot (but be careful as it can burn) into parcels by placing them on top of a wine bottle and gently trying to fold in half, pinching the sides. It is very easy to tear the biscuit so take your time and be gentle.

Repeat 3 more times to create 4 biscuits.

Bring a pan of water to a simmer and place a bowl above (make sure the bowl doesn't touch the water).

Add 150g white chocolate to the bowl and melt over the water. When melted, add 4tbs single cream. Slice open a vanilla pod lengthways and scrape out the seeds and add the seeds to the chocolate. Add a gelatine leaf to water and leave for 3 minutes, then add 1 pre-soaked gelatine sheet to the chocolate and mix well. Remove from heat.

When the chocolate has cooled and has almost set, spoon 2 - 3 tsp into each biscuit parcel. It is important the chocolate is not too runny or it won't fill the parcel, it will just leak out.

To serve, cut 2 strawberries into quarters and chop 4 blackberries into halves. Add 2 quarters of strawberry and 2 halves of the blackberry to each parcel and then the mint and thyme leaves. Sprinkle over icing sugar.

Strawberry and vanilla cheese cake (8 people)

You will need:

3 gelatine sheets, 500g Philadelphia cheese, 2tbs crème fraiche, 1 tsp vanilla extract, 80g butter, 125g shortbread, 50g digestive biscuits, 450g Tiptree strawberries (or any very high quality strawberries you can get), 75g caster sugar, 2 vanilla pods, 1 egg

Cut the 2 vanilla pods lengthways and remove the seeds using a knife. Add the empty vanilla pods and seeds to a sauce pan and add 3tbs water, 1tsp vanilla essence and 50g caster sugar. Cook on lowest heat possible for at least 15 minutes, stirring occasionally to mix the sugar into the water. Turn off heat and leave for 30 minutes to allow the flavours to infuse further.

Pre-heat oven to 180°C. Crumble 50g digestive biscuits and 125g shortbread (some small lumps are good – you don't want a powder) by putting the biscuits into a sandwich bag and use a rolling pin to break them down.

Gently melt 80g butter in a pan, and then add the biscuit mixture and remove from heat. Stir until all the butter is absorbed and well distributed in the biscuit mixture.

Pour mixture into a cake tin (ideally with a removable bottom and about 8inches in diameter) and spread evenly but very firmly (it has to be compacted – use the back of a large spoon as it has a bigger surface area) and put in oven until cooked (the base will appear to bubble when it's done) – about 10 minutes. Remove from oven and allow to cool.

After the vanilla pods have infused, removed the stalks and add 1 beaten egg, 300g Philadelphia and 1tbs crème fraiche. Slowly and gently spoon over the cooled biscuit mixture. Return to the oven and cook on 180C until it looks like the top is set approximately 15 minutes (or until the edges just start to brown). To test, lightly touch the centre with your finger, it should be dry and resistant to your touch. Remove from oven and allow to cool.

In a sauce pan, add the 450g washed and topped Tiptree strawberries and 25g caster sugar and cook on low/medium heat for 30 minutes, stirring occasionally.

Meanwhile soak 3 gelatine sheets in water for 5 minutes, squeeze out any liquid and add to the pan and allow to melt. Turn off heat, then, add 1tbs crème fraiche and 200g Philadelphia. Use a blender and blend into a smooth sauce. Gently pour the fruit cheese cake mixture onto the vanilla cheese cake and allow to set in the fridge. Serve after 6 hours.

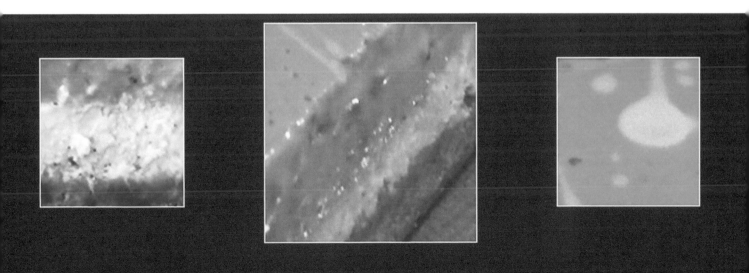

Mango and toffee meringues (4 - 8 people)

You will need:

4 egg whites, 140g caster sugar, 1 peeled mango with ½ of it chopped into 5mm x 5mm cubes, 400g condensed milk, 8 edible rice paper sheets, 1tsp pomegranate molasses, ¼ tsp chopped parsley leaves, ¼ tsp chopped coriander and juice from ¼ Satsuma orange

Prepare in advance:

Pre-heat oven to 140°C.

Whisk 2 eggs whites with an electric whisk until they form peaks. Turn the speed up and slowly add 70g of caster sugar. Continue for another 30 seconds or until stiff and glossy. Transfer the egg whites into a piping bag and shape into small meringue cones on top of the edible rice paper, approximately 1inch in diameter and equally tall. Very carefully lightly brown one side of the meringue with a blow torch. Repeat this process with the remaining 2 egg whites and 70g caster sugar.

Add to the oven and cook for about 30 (until lightly caramel coloured), turn heat down to 120°C and cook for another 15 minutes. Then turn off the heat and leave in the oven until oven is cold (or overnight).

In a pan of boiling water, add a 400g can of condensed milk and gently simmer it for 3 – 3 ½ hours (pierce the can once to allow any steam out to prevent the can from exploding; actually I never pierce it and it's never exploded but it's not worth the risk that I advise others to do the same as me). Top the water up as necessary. Allow to cool before opening.

15 minutes before this dish is required, take 2 meringues and spread a thin layer of the condensed milk (which is now 'Dulce de Leche' after the cooking process) over each. Place 5-6 mango pieces on one of the toffee layers and then press the other meringue against it to create a sandwich. If you make these too early, the meringues will go soggy.

Boil the remaining mango with 1tbs water. When boiling, turn off from heat and puree. Stir in 1tsp pomegranate molasses and ¼ tsp chopped parsley leaves, ¼ tsp chopped coriander and juice from ¼ Satsuma orange. Mix well.

Place several meringues on a plate to serve with a light dribble of the mango puree around the plate.

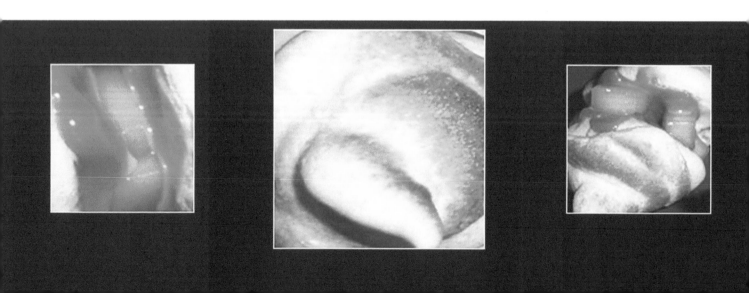

Hazelnut and honey parfait, rose jellies and vanilla caramels (4 people)

You will need:

300ml whipped cream, 4 eggs, 100g honey, 100ml Frangelico (hazelnut liqueur), 50ml rose syrup, 1 gelatine sheet, 1 vanilla pod, 20g white caster sugar

Prepare in advance:

Whip 4 egg whites until they form stiff peaks and transfer to a large bowl. Then, whip 300ml of whipping cream until very thick and gently fold into the egg whites.

Beat 4 egg yolks until thick and gently fold into the mixture.

In a saucepan, boil 100g honey and 100ml Frangelico for 2 minutes, and allow to cool.

Very gently combine the honey to the eggs whites, yolks and cream.

Use an ice cube tray to shape. Drop a spoonful of cream mixture into each container and add another ½ tsp Frangelico and 1tsp honey (which will sink to the bottom). Freeze. The rest can be frozen (use an ice cream maker) and used like ice cream throughout the week.

Soak 1 gelatine sheet in water for 5 minutes. Add 50ml rose syrup and 110ml water to a pan and bring to a simmer and add the gelatine sheet and mix well. Allow to cool and fill an ice cube tray. Freeze.

Empty the rose jellies from their containers. Then, return to their containers and put into the fridge and allow to defrost. We do this whilst the jellies are frozen to ensure they don't break (which they do when soft). The parfait needs to remain frozen.

Add to a frying pan the seeds from ½ vanilla pod and 20g caster sugar. Cook on high and when turning golden, turn off heat. Hopefully, by the time it starts to cool it will be golden. When the caramel is cool enough to touch, put the tip of a spoon in, stir around and gently lift up taking a 'strand' of caramel with you. This is the vanilla caramel. Snap at the length desired.

To serve, place 3 jellies on one side of the pate, 3 parfait domes on the other (mirroring each other) and a vanilla caramel in the middle, slightly askew so it doesn't look parallel.